Strides

reflections on 6 acres

by Laurence Carr

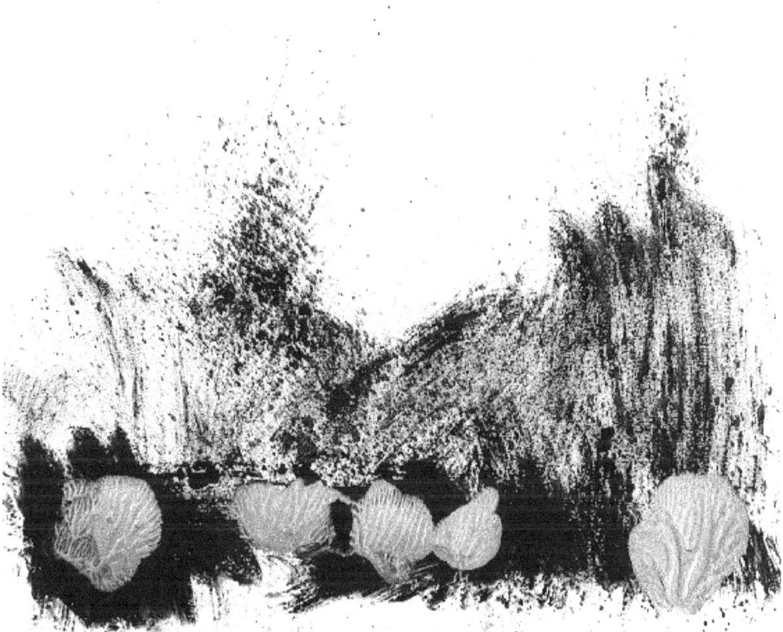

artwork by Edward M. O'Hara

CAPS Press and Lightwoodpress

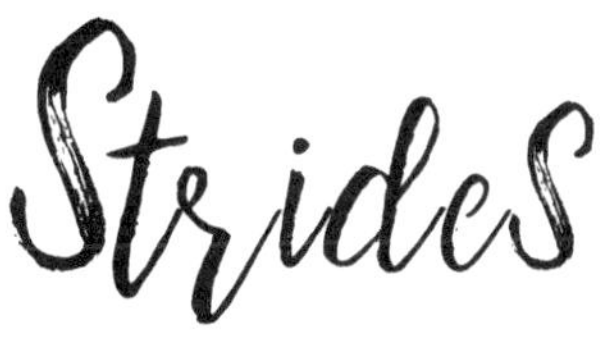

reflections on 6 acres

by Laurence Carr

artwork by Edward M. O'Hara

CAPS Press and Lightwoodpress

Published by CAPS Press and Lightwoodpress

Contact: larrycarr521@gmail.com

www.Lightwoodpress.com

Artwork by Edward M. O'Hara
Images copyright by the artist, 2024
www.oharaart.com
@edohara.art

Book design by Slavo Kiss and Edward M. O'Hara

FIRST EDITION
ISBN- 978-1-734410-7-8

Acknowledgements

I want to thank my wife, Kay, for being my partner on this journey, for her constant support, and for her wonderful quilts. And to virtual friends during the creation of this book: David Appelbaum, Power Boothe, Garrison Botts, Bill Burnett, Joan Grant, Stephen Hoffman, Michaeljohn McGann, Jess Nadelman, Jeanette Smith, and to my brother, Gary. And special thanks to the members of my writing group: Susan Chute, Stephanie JT Russell (Pina), Tim Brennan, and Kim Ellis for their support and literary skills to help this work see the light of day.

"Perimeter" first appeared in *Clerestory* magazine.
"I've Heard It Said" first appeared in
Deep Wild: Writing From the Back Country

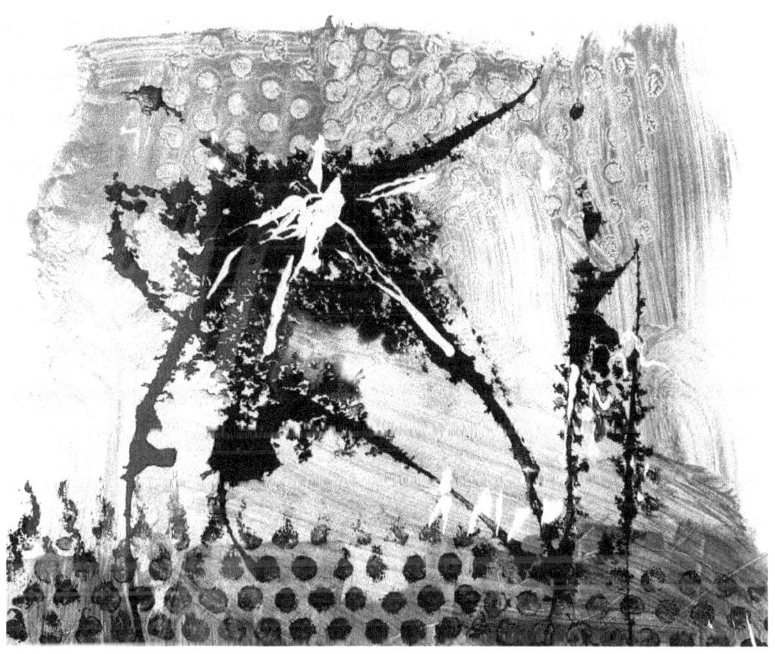

Table of Contents

Preface

Another subtitle for the Strides collection is "a year in review."
Most of the writings came about over a two-year period
between the second half of 2021 and into the fall of 2022.
A few were written later. I hesitate to label these "pandemic
poems" as none of them directly address the grueling,
demanding time we passed through.

However, during these months, I set aside portions of nearly
every day to walk through the several acres surrounding the
1820s farmhouse in New York's Hudson Valley where my wife
and I live. I observed—not to simply look at but to take things
in. I found time to make notes of soil, leaves, rocks, stumps,
trees, birds, animal tracks and scat. I examined the human
shaping of the land: rock walls, stick piles, foundations, and
the generations of detritus left behind, once buried but now
heaved up by spring thaws or fall torrential rains. I examined
shards of glass and pottery, rusty bedsprings, a pot and
pan, marbles and a host of other stuff, once possessed then
abandoned or lost.

As difficult as it was to be confined for the better part of that
time, I now value it. Nature gives us different eyes, a gift given,
exactly when a gift is needed.

Soon after, Eddie O'Hara and I discovered each other's art
and decided to collaborate on this project. I thank him for his
deep insight into the natural world and how his images are
companions to my words.

Rocks
Breathe in
Flatten earth
Float beneath sky
Hold their treasures close
It takes a hard rain to open your hearts.

deer scat
cat scat
at night they scat
their songs scatological

Perimeter (in 3)

1.

It takes 650 steps to walk the perimeter. Not the full perimeter,
but just the one I walk. Sometimes it takes 725 steps and
sometimes 645, depending on my stride, a corner cut,
or a hundred other deep distractions.

The two of us have lived together with this land but were never
comfortable with "Ownership." We're transients here, like the
Saxtons were in 1820. We're names on a page scrolling from
past to future. Until the world decides on a major renovation.

I usually don't climb the hill behind us, called Illinois Mountain
by the locals, the wooded rise that leads to a rocky ridge.
Named in the long time long ago by someone who took the
secret with them.

2.

I've searched for the word that describes our presence here:
custodian (a little too middle school)
concierge (a little too French farce)
keeper (too zoo oppressive)
overseer (no, for too many reasons)
agent (too snarky Hollywood)
guardian (too Marvel Comics)
watchman (nothing with "man" and too back-alley noir)
warden (too Trollope)
steward (good but everyone will think that's our name)
ostiary (who knows this anymore?)
curator? Perhaps a good fit. We curate here. Maintain, restore,
reuse the old: replacing not with flossy
but with what the house agrees,

3.

I walk the perimeter a couple times a week. Counting steps but
often losing count halfway. Because of that leaf or this stone.
This stone, this one. Here.

Pushed along by a passing glacier or ascended from our
molten core. Vomited up from inner belly rumblings. Catching
a lift from a meteor taxi in a great stone shower.

A lost memory now, the past seeps back underground.
I stoop to pick you up and the perimeter walk moves on.
In silence. Still pebbles run deep.

The stone warms in my hand. Warmth from body heat or from
the remnants of lava dreams. Unknown and then along the
way, we find a place to stop. A mutual agreement. I set the
stone down at a place of trust, familiar but new. And there
you'll stay until Nature or another one, the one who isn't me
takes it on another world-class whirl-wind tour.
A circle of memory.

The stone has shifted its position in the crusty ether. The
land is altered. I've been revised. Returned. To walk the new
perimeter tomorrow.

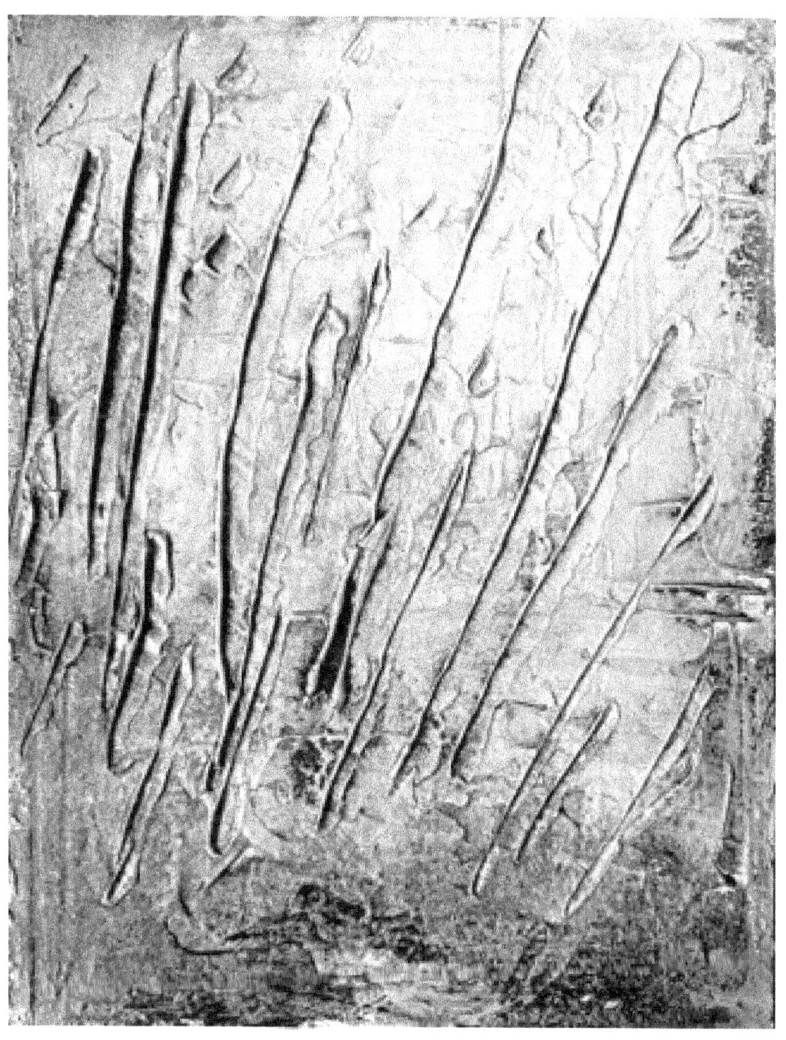

I've Heard It Said

You'll never know another person till you walk their path.
Sound advice I suppose.

I walk out onto the snow to find my footsteps from the day
before then place my boot soles into theirs. Up the hill, across
the rise, step by step we walk together, sole to sole, trying for
the life of me to understand that person I was yesterday.

But he's no longer here. A foreigner now, some wandering
nomad with only impressions left in the snow.

Stand 1

glass globe snow
shakes through the trees
incandescent in the moonlight
each flake a ghostly raindrop

Stand 2

the blackened sticks
nearly disappear
their peeling bark rubs
a chant of snow songs

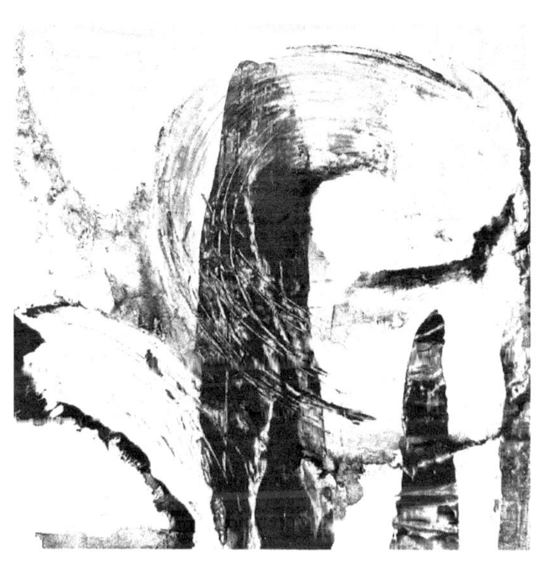

Making Inroads

It's a chore for all seasons. To work The Path.
To help it find its passageway.

The work calls for clearing fallen limbs in the spring. In
summer laying mounds of wood chips. In fall, the raking,
the hide and seek with oak and maple leaves. But now with
January's foot-high snowfall, The Path has gone missing.
Vamoosed to warmer climes, no doubt, without a word.

It's meandered far afield and after weeks away sends me a
text with a "wish you were here" typed in annoying caps and a
selfie—it's lolling on some sunny beach, its shifty toes
playing in the sand then ending with a "maybe see you in the
spring xo" and closing with emojis that smell of April soil.

I texted back. "You're young and need to wander but know that
all paths lead back here. You can come home again."

Chez Crow

I dust off the snow on the "critter rock" to lay out our table scraps. Bones picked clean from yesterday's feast are tossed unburied on the chalk white ground.

The crows are choosy but answer when I call. I "caw" but never know if I'm offending or inviting them to belly up for bones and gristle, a bit of fatty skin seasoned with au jus or the remains of the cats' seafood platter licked and then ignored.

The menu at Chez Crow features seasonal specials. Turkey vultures like roadside dining. Eat and run. Fresher meals, the recently deceased mouse or vole, a plaything that the cats chase then sniff and then ignore, then served up on a dustpan on the shoulder of the road. Hawks prefer their meals tartar and seek out dining companions in woodsy bistros. They arrive uninvited and are content with carry out.

The cat watches with her Charon Cheshire smile awaiting what the universe will waft her way. With always an eye to the skies.

Stand 3

deer tracks
stalk themselves
in concentric circles
looking for clues

a mystery train hoofs
through snow
through woods
that watch and wait

Stand 4

spruce and hemlock
greener now than in July

forgive my eye that overlooked you
until this snowbound day
these woods will soon become
your perfect summer hideout

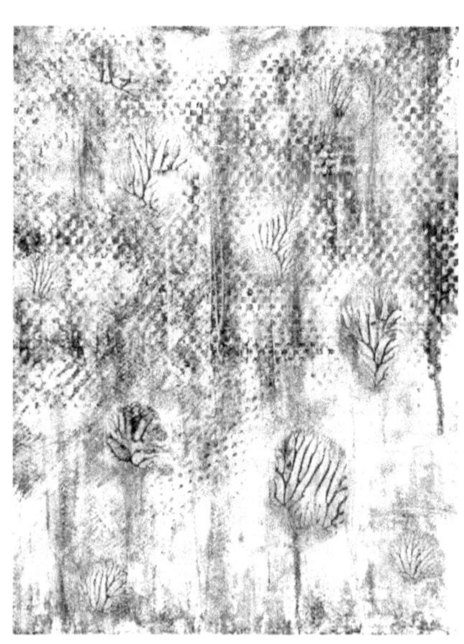

march omen

warm winds flutter the flesh
and refresh the forward path

rumors of hidden fortunes
stir budding wealth
in growing agitation

The Count

No matter how many times you count the chickens you'll always get a different number. You'll count 7 then 11 then 13 then 20; they're moving targets to the eye, a kaleidoscope of image.

Feathered forms that circle like rogue planets in and out of orbit. There's something celestial about them and about their mythic eggs, both sacred and profane.

They've harnessed the complex and the simple and live where time is meaningless and numbers don't add up.

Permanence

Outside the permanence of latitudes and through these times
uncertain the east west stick fence remains. A retaining wall,
but memory is lost from what it separates or holds in place. A
great dark whale of broken boughs whose ribs no longer rise
or fall with the breath of snow.

This stickpile fence, weighed down by years of bugs, disease
and snowstorms, by windy hail. And after holding on and
out it disappears so easily from eyes no longer seeing it. And
becomes a row of antimatter—

But in the long game it endures and will never reach that place
where it becomes no matter.

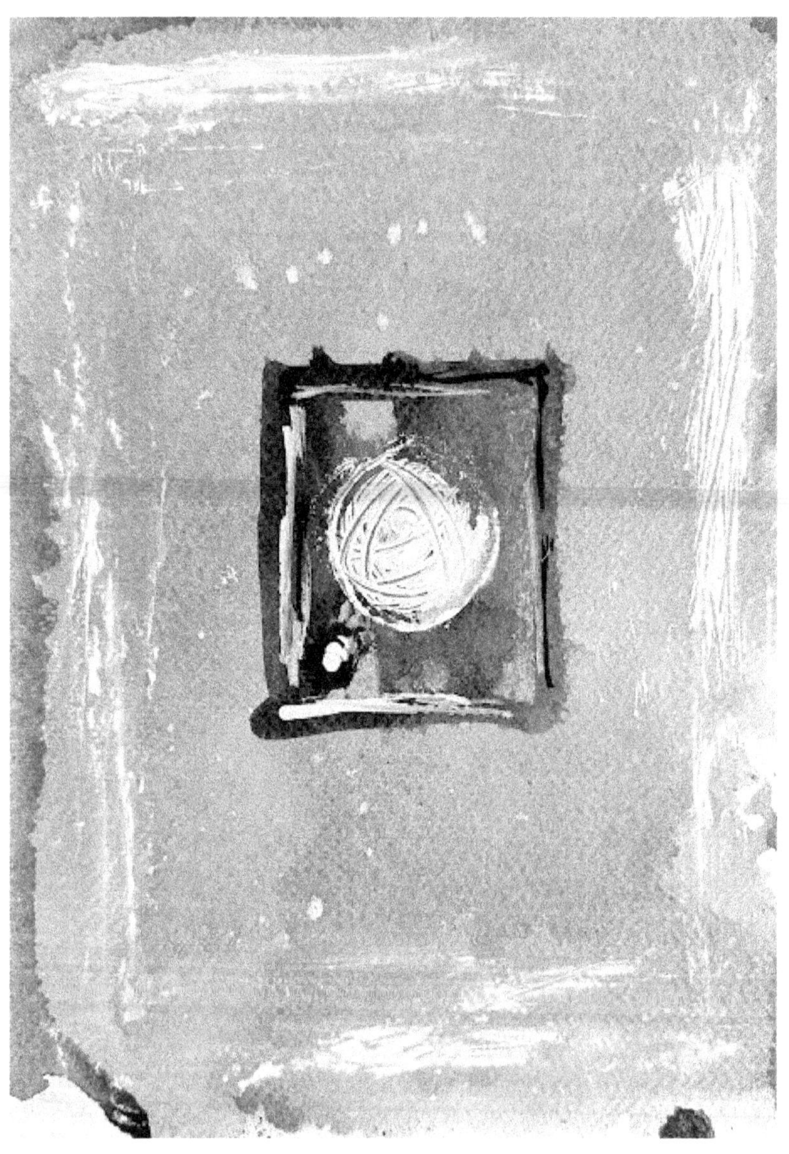

Walkabout

The artist and writer walked the land. They broke their silence with a word or phrase or sometimes a small gesture that brought a guttural hum of mutual insight.

They walked among rocks and beside rock walls, past trees and over fallen trunks and logs broken down to iron-colored earth. They picked up two branches that became walking stick companions.

Then headed to the barn to observe the metal cooking pot hanging from a nail on the outside wall. A pot discarded but not thrown away. A pot that still had a dozen uses: to hold soil, compost, to collect those shards of glass and crockery that the spring thaw heaves up. It could catch water that drips off the barn's lone gutter. Or could hold another discarded pot.

Nearby, leaning against the paint-flaked barn wall, a metal basket, a rectangle of woven wire pitted to silver-gray. Retired but not tossed out. A basket that still could be used to organize those jars or bottles that made their way to the barn, or those containers of used oil from the mowers awaiting the yearly journey to hazardous waste. Or could nest another discarded wire basket.

The two wanderers pick up the basket and hang it on the same nail, covering but not obscuring the dented metal pot hanging inside it. Basket and pot as equals, sharing the space.

The two objects begin to speak, to converse with each other, to the barn and to the wanderers. Each holds its own energy and from these, a third energy radiates.

A rectangle of corona around a silver moon.

Two unknown planets now in syzygy never seen before.

A pot and basket hanging on a barn wall,
an imprint of ourselves.

Stand 5

her ice storms glisten haute couture

designs of silver white run up and
down the walkway

but her fashions will soon drop out of season
and she'll cloister in her workroom sketching out
next year's winter line

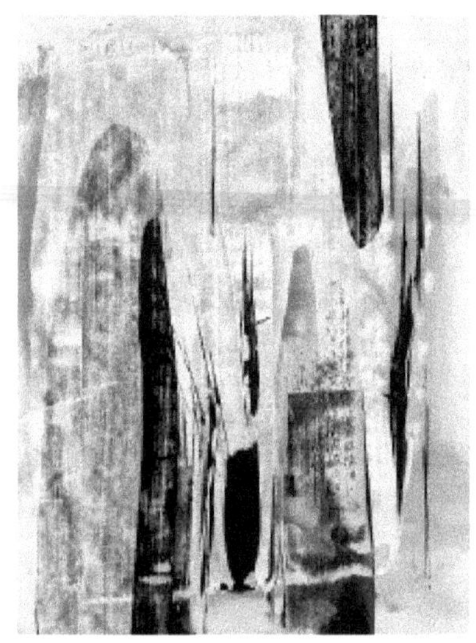

Stand 6

the stone wall cascades a vein
of silver sunlit ice

you prospectors, don't delay
the spring thaw will roll in
before you know it

Wake Robin*

Wake robin arouses and justifies herself.
She resurrects from the thawed earth,
breathes the world and takes her turn.

another
self
aware
awoke

*flower: trillium erectum, in the family Melanthiaceae,
nurturing the myth of the red breast of the robin,
announcing the coming of spring.

birding in spring

thru a lifeline branch
peeks an instant now/not now
leaf star shepherd hides
eyes that meet/not meet
a never quite observer
of a seen/unseen still presence

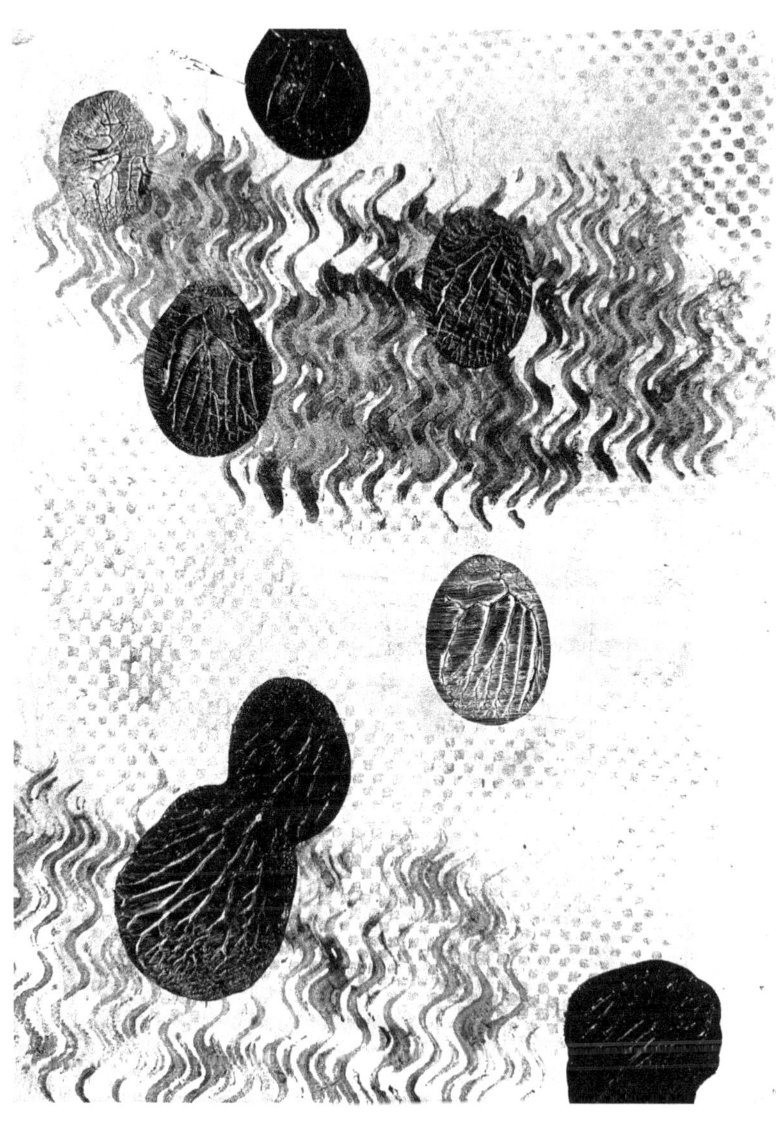

Ground Glass (in 3)

1.

There was no garbage pickup in the old days. And if you had
an extra acre, you dug a pit and this became the family dump,
an archeology of ancestry, once removed.

The terminal for nearly everything that couldn't be refitted
or reworn—bones and rotten vegetables, broken jugs and
glassware. Bent utensils the pig had chewed and decided not
to swallow. Clothes kept as hand-me-downs turn to oil rags
and after that half-life are pitched.

The contents seep into the earth layer by layer, year by year.
Perhaps some dirt was thrown over to hide the stuff of daily
life, a burial of sorts but with no marker, headstone or carved
inscription. And never exhumed till now.

2.

It's a cloudless sunny day today. A cliché of pleasantry. I walk my walk around the grounds. And here and there see the remains of bottles, jars and crockery, tossed into the ageless pit by generations long gone.

The winter thaw heaves up these relics from where they've rested comfortably. Slowly erupting in early spring. My April job is to pick up what's revealed and toss them in a bucket to recycle. Shards of glass and pottery, some dulled by age, some still razor sharp. A spiky piece could cut a paw or hoof so my daily pickup chore continues, but never seems to end. It's a mythic labor to find every shard that's been embedded all these years.

3.

Thoughts turn to other times and places where shattered glass lay grounded. Bricks from anonymous hands smash nighttime storefronts scrolled with yellow stars and sky-high buildings explode from kidnapped planes riding on a cloudless, sunny day just like today.

Distant memories circle my solitude. And within my grasp the remains emerge from an earth that never forgets.

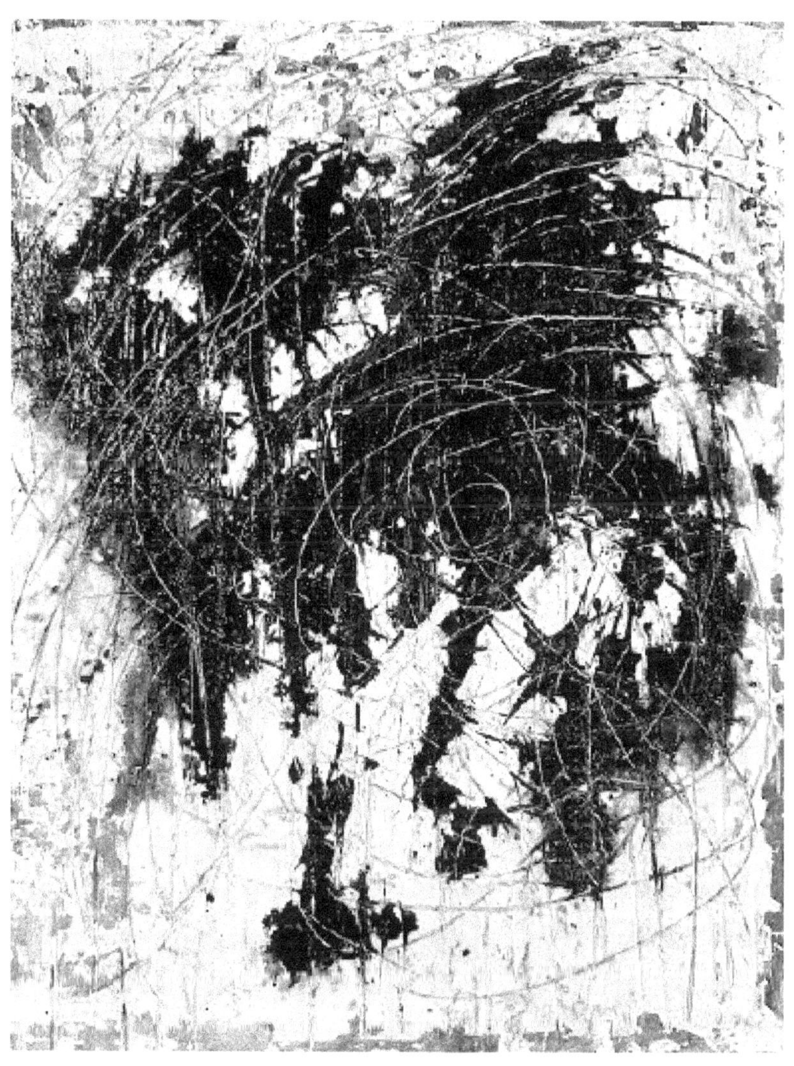

Stand 7

gray clouds
give the low hanging sun
a silver mask so it can
pretend to be the moon

Stand 8

lichens greening gray
move at the pace of stars
the age of each their secret

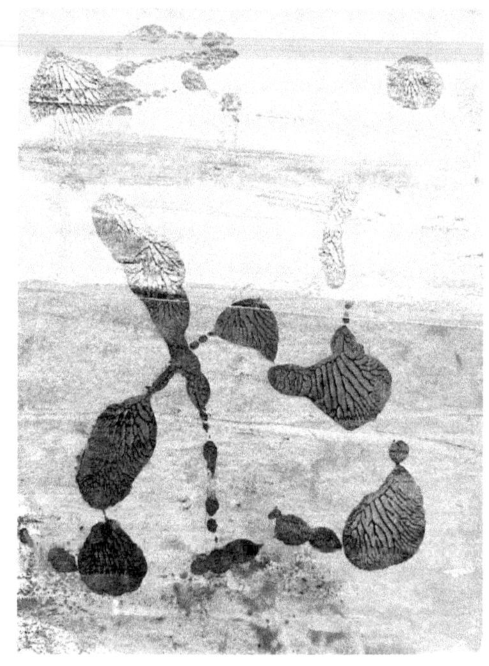

Border Crossing (in 2)

1.

The chickens come by but not to roost. This isn't their home,
but the place they've come to occupy. They live across a span
of unraked leaves, over the stickfence and through a run of
uncleared woods.

They billet here three times a day to rustle through our
unmulched leaves, scratch through our moss and compost,
pecking for our grubs and ticks and things only they can see.

The cat knows it's best to keep her distance. They far
outnumber her. Last year there were five, then ten, now
eighteen by last count. And not bantam sized.

They keep a watchful eye on everything. We welcomed them
at first. Thought it better to accommodate.

The cool breeze fluffs them up, encasing them in downy vests
like flak jackets. And headed by a rooster,
tall and in command.

He cuts the others slack to forage where they want as long
as they return. At first, they edged the property, just beyond
the border, then day by day they explored further, two on
surveillance, checking out what was safe, then expanding,
taking ground.

They're often out of sight, rearranging paths, annexing a little
more each day, hoping we won't notice.

I've cleaned up their droppings, wearing gloves and armed
with a garden trowel: a nuisance but I'm told their dried and
cured manure makes good compost. Is this their final offer?

2.

They're on the hunt to appropriate our resources— ones
we'd concede to establish a treaty between two sovereign
neighbors. But a policy statement has never been proposed.

Perhaps they're apolitical; when they flap their wings to cover
ground, their ruffled feathers left and right seem equal. But
still, it would be good to know where they stand. Sometimes,
perched on both legs then on one. And their language,
both foreign and domestic. Sometimes we'd like to open
communication, but have we missed our chance?

We've accommodated, turned our heads, but will it be enough?
Yesterday, they were on the welcome mat outside
the back door.

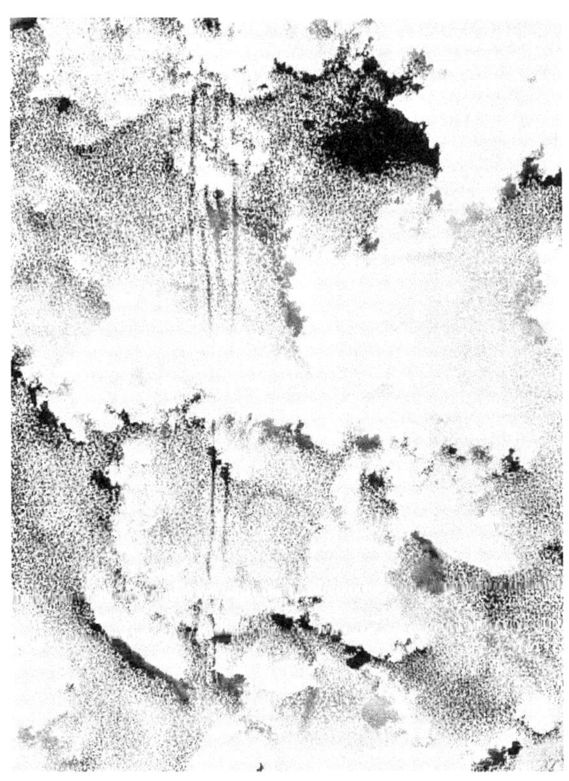

Stand 9

on a locust tree
a jutting twig gave me
second glance

a walking stick,
half bug, half twig
hidden from intruders

we stand eye to eye
both without
a predatory thought

Stand 10

there's talk of a
fisher and a bobcat

tales as tall as spruces
words become footprints
visible to those who
track them

Placement (in 2)

1.

He brought up wood from the basement that had rested there
for generations. Why today remains a mystery. Things catch
the eye after years of invisibility.

On the way to the stickfence, the debate ensues. These old,
milled beams, some hand-hewn, in foot-long lengths are of
a different stock and lineage, from a different time and place
from the sticks that stack the stickfence.

These stove-length beams weren't wind-blown limbs or
branches chipped away by the downies and red bellies, then
gathered by the armload and piled onto the makeshift fence
with thought-out randomness.

These beams should live out their days up in the woods to get
to know themselves and over time with their fallen cousins,
mulch together to blanket the ground.
A better end to begin again.

On the way to the woods, a beam dropped to lean against the
well cover and soon disappeared from sight and mind just as
the others had before, soon to become part of the well-cover,
a part of its own landscape.

2.

One day, a season down the road, at weeding time, he stoops
by the well to pull an unknown plant. Unknown to him but
not to itself.

Nearby, the forgotten beam is seen again. He lifts it up and
underneath, a large, brown warty toad stares back at him.
Crouching—poised to attack. Or silent, still and petrified. No
breath, invisible, a piece of rock-hard wood. Two living statues.
Man and Toad. They read each other's battlelines. Their
ancient laws unscroll, each in their separate tongues.

But then breath comes. Dark clouds disperse.

With a stone he props the beam to make a roof. He trusts he
wouldn't spring and spit his fabled acid. He trusts the roof will
not collapse on him.

He finds scraps from a broken crate. Two walls are added. A
toad house roadhouse. He eats the insects in the herb garden.
He watches him from his window. Soon enough, time will
move them on.

gaming

stone covers moss
moss covers stone

stone hides moss
moss hides stone

each a seasoned player
at the top of their game

whose origin is clouded in
an ancient past
its finish line unknown

where no time outs
or overtime
no tie-breaks
or countdown clock
can intercede

like the games we played
in our infant days
when we were stone and moss

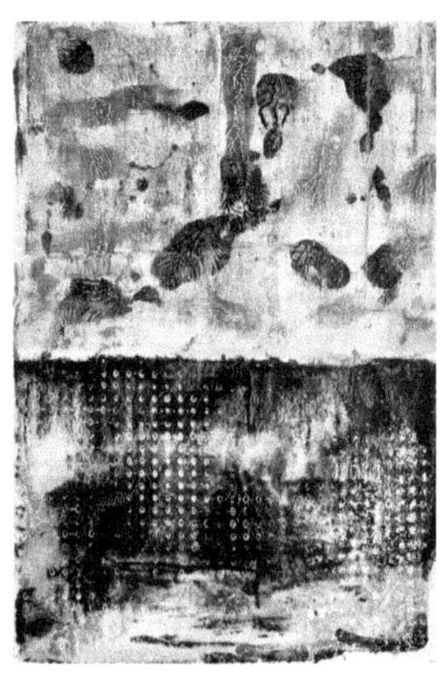

Stand 11

a window embedded
  in the stone wall
    still holds four shards
      of pane inside its broken frame
        and memories of land's end

Stand 12

my walking stick
  a sturdy broken branch
    takes me up the hill

    i'm a tripod with a camera's eye
      recording what's unseen
        from down below

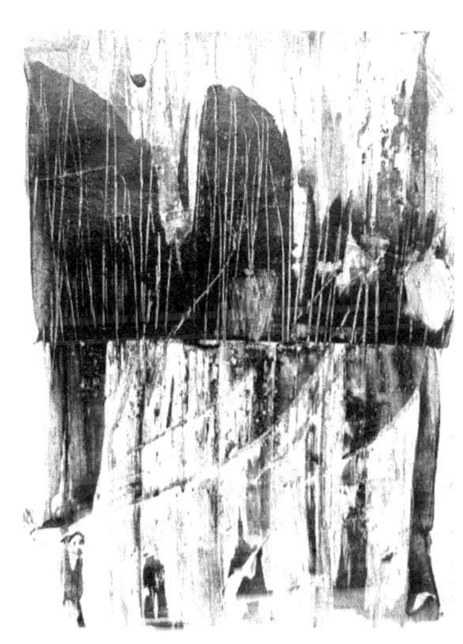

All the Marbles (in 3)

1.

A second cat's eye marble emerged from the moss-covered gully halfway up the hill. I add it to the aggies, the blue, and the caramel swirl I found nearby over the past 10 years.

They now sit on the porch windowsill not far from their burial ground. Buried in a childhood ritual? A childhood revenge? Or did they escape of their own volition, lose themselves like umbrellas or acquaintances?

Tired of their underground life, they surface to our world, helped by a spring thaw or the autumn torrential rain.

2.

Memory washes over: an elementary recess on a warm fall
day after lunchtime with its peanut butter and jelly or bologna
wedged between a sponge of bread with quartered apples
a little past their prime. Their smell permeates the air, our
clothes and hair.

Through the schoolhouse doors around to the side to the
earthen track, between the red brick wall and cement sidewalk
the games begin. From a schoolpants' pocket, a cloth or
leather pouch shakes out half a dozen marbles then the glass
shooter—his prize possession.

A ring is scratched in the dirt with a popsicle stick, as close to
a perfect circle as the hand and eye can etch. The marbles are
tossed inside its rim. The shooter marble, held between the
bent forefinger and thumbnail, awaiting the flick to propel it
through the ring, aiming to hit another's marble and knock it
out. The opponent's marbles—the winning prize
to win the day.

3.

where glass-eyed spheres
sit in polished Grecian heads
where cats stare up at
David's cracked imperfect monolith
and Elgin stones await their fate
where chisels croon Carrara tunes
where I dream I dwell in marble halls

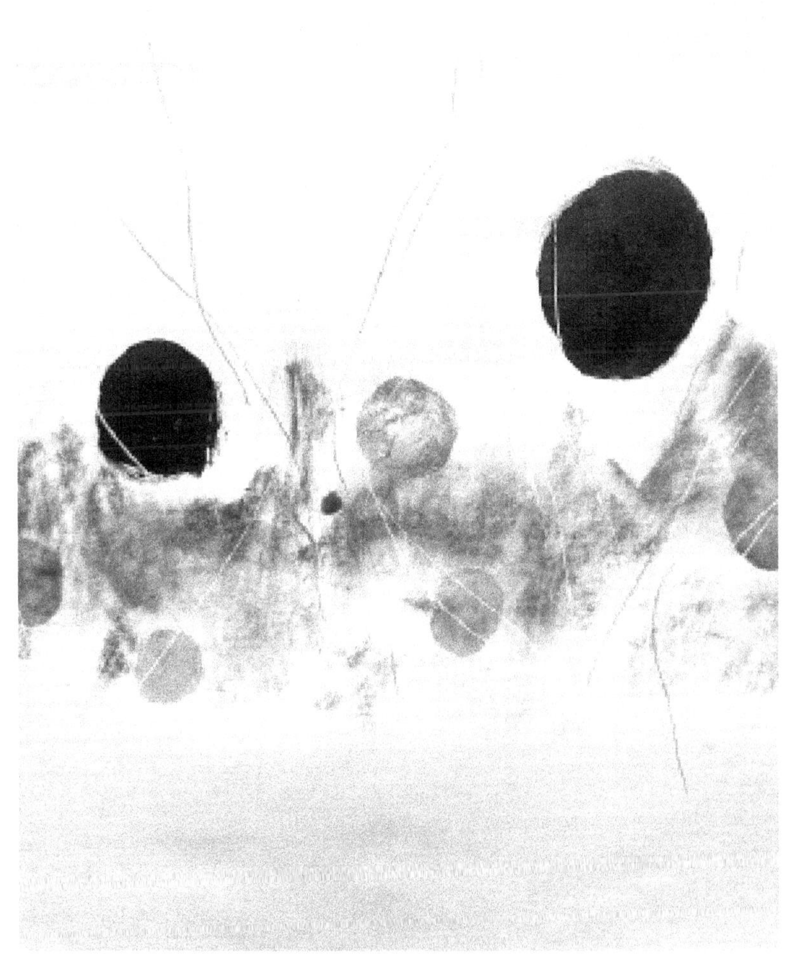

Capped
(Picus Niger Maximus Capite Rubro)

He (I assume you're a "he" after looking at your
online mugshot.) wobbled on the feeder but found
his tree-legs on the trunk of the old maple.

Pileatus from the Latin "capped".

Your hideout is the woods and in 20 years has allowed
3 sightings. Each one, I assume, a different you. That is
the prayer— that you live on—surrounded by the woods
that have been yours for longer than we know.

There's majesty in you, so unlike the cartoon Woody—
the trickster bird not the cowboy.
You fly with Pilates energy with a wingspan wide enough to
embrace us. When I was young we called you— "pie-lated"—
the dessert and not the endless number.

There's joy and sadness watching you— such joy in our
encounter, then a heartthrob that you could go the way of
your ivory-billed cousin. If we take away your homeland—
when and not if unless we're vigilant.

Return to us when you feel safe—your visit can be brief—
just long enough to know you're still around. That you
endure when those of us observing are never quite sure
our presence is secure.

Leaf Raking

Repetitive motion should bring on contemplation, but here
in late autumn, blank stares wed with blanker thoughts. Over
and over, the rake's vertical strokes with its thin-tined oars
with no coxswain or finish line in sight.

Leaves uncounted sweep onto tarpaulin rugs then roll up like
Cleopatra gifted to a Roman tribune.

A dried and shriveled thin façade of former lives is hauled
and dumped into the leaf ditch or mounded in the leaf corral
awaiting snow drifts who will shroud them out of sight.

We stand inside fogging the window with anticipation like at
a children's birthday party dumbfounded at the magician's
grand finale.

And with that same willing disbelief, the abracadabra of
springtime sun lifts the white linen to unveil a modest bank of
compost, dark and rich. A conjurer's trick that will
never be revealed.

Stand 13

the red barn flakes
off color a melt
away from memory

barns turn to
ghosts but take the
centuries they need
content to live their
in between

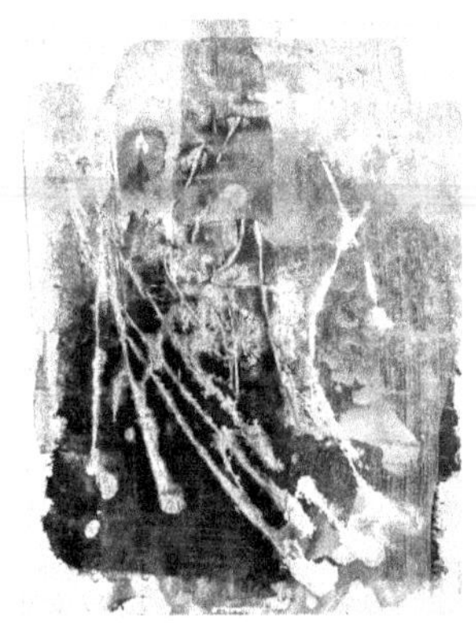

Stand 14

tree watches the
stick fence and
understands the
weight of time to
turn itself to earth

rock watches the
stone wall crack and
understands the
weight of time to
turn itself to dust.

Life Raft

A rafter of turkeys passes through across the road to
the wetland. A line of poults marches quickstep close
behind eyes wide to spot the bobcat or coyote.

We never see their flight, but have seen them rafting in
a tree, wings tightly folded, neckless heads perched on
shadowed forms, eyes focused for the hawk or eagle.

They start to disappear when leaves begin to fall.
Their saunter, a quilted drunkard's path breaks into
a sprint, like they're trying to outrun their predators,
which, in fact, they are.

Necks jerk around to spot the autumn hunter, the latest
blunderbuss in hand, stalking the woods in combat boots,
who never quite attains a pilgrim's progress

And when the rafter finds safe nest do they fold their wings
and pray the prayer of native birds on native land to live
another season here?—then pray for their cousins heaped
on November Thursday's dinner plates.

Aviary (in 2)

1.

The chickens peck and scratch their way across what seems
every inch of ground looking for clues to an unsolved crime.
The raft of turkeys follows with old school eyes. They strut
slowly, as if waiting for something only they know will arrive.

And here comes the Dodo with Martha, the Passenger Pigeon,
and a chorus of Bachman's Warblers. A Laughing Owl flies
low nodding to the Great Auk looking up. A Carolina Parakeet
in a mid-air dance with a Saint Helena Dove. All swirling
around, an aviary long hidden outside the frame now
surrounding me in plain sight. Each one distinct,
each a stroke of color.

2.

An arc of archeopteryxes swoops down. Just passing through.
They used to call this home, but now they find more
benevolent climes. But maybe our warmth
will let them reconsider.

A tureen of pterodactyls glides into view, like kites with
no strings attached. The gusts of autumn figure-eight them
over treetops then plunge them close enough to feel their
skin-tight wings.

And the one who watches over this, perches on a boulder
half-way up the hill. One of the old outcrops incised with
glyphs telling of the day after days.

We're here together in this place, among the glacial stones
and lichens. The departed who never part from here.
Each one each the other's memory.

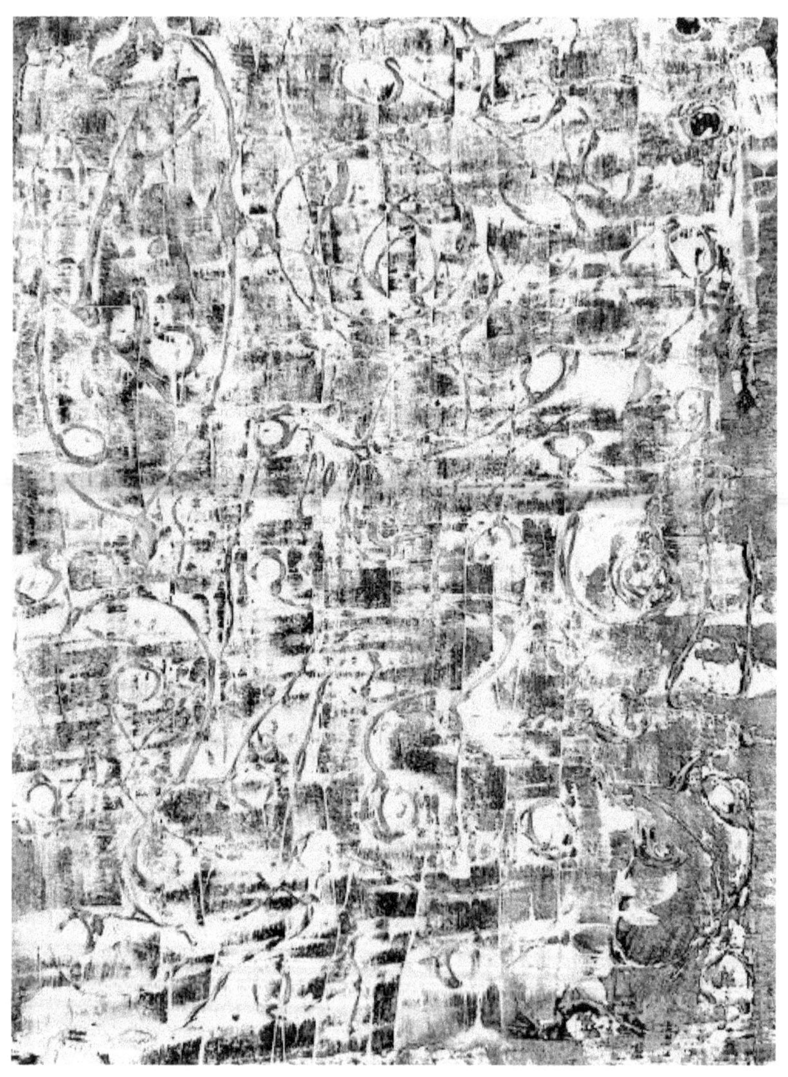

deep horizon

the autumn wren in a sunset cloak
seduced by southern winds

the autumn wren cloaks in darkness
her compass needle trembles

the autumn wren charts the course
far from snow gust breath

the autumn wren airmails herself
to latitudes all-knowing

the fallen pine crazy glues onto a sheath of winter quiet

she ends her century long study of the stairway sky

to begin her deep horizon contemplation

So Many So Much

There haven't been this many woolly bears in years.
At least what my eye is counting. Cloaked in black and
brown— caterpillars of things to come.

The myth is that the longer the brown sections, the milder
the winter. The more black, the more severe.

I see some with equal stripes, then some in traditional black,
never out of style.

Some don coats of fuzzy brown, an unnamable color
but a hue high-end designers relish to define.

Would they think Woolly Bear Brown too common?

They crawl across the bluestone walk and the crushed rock
that imbeds the driveway. I pick them up and they curl like
cats on laps, then place them near the plants or on the mulch.

Am I doing them a favor or have I just upset the great,
grand scheme of Nature?
Am I the helpmate or the hindrance?

Can one be both in a single breath?
And do these alternating currents pass through us,
day by day until we lose our charge and the verdict's
finally read?
Do poems ultimately matter?

Or is ephemera just that? A fleeting thought speeding toward
the great and grand unknown?

There've been so many Woolly Bears this fall.

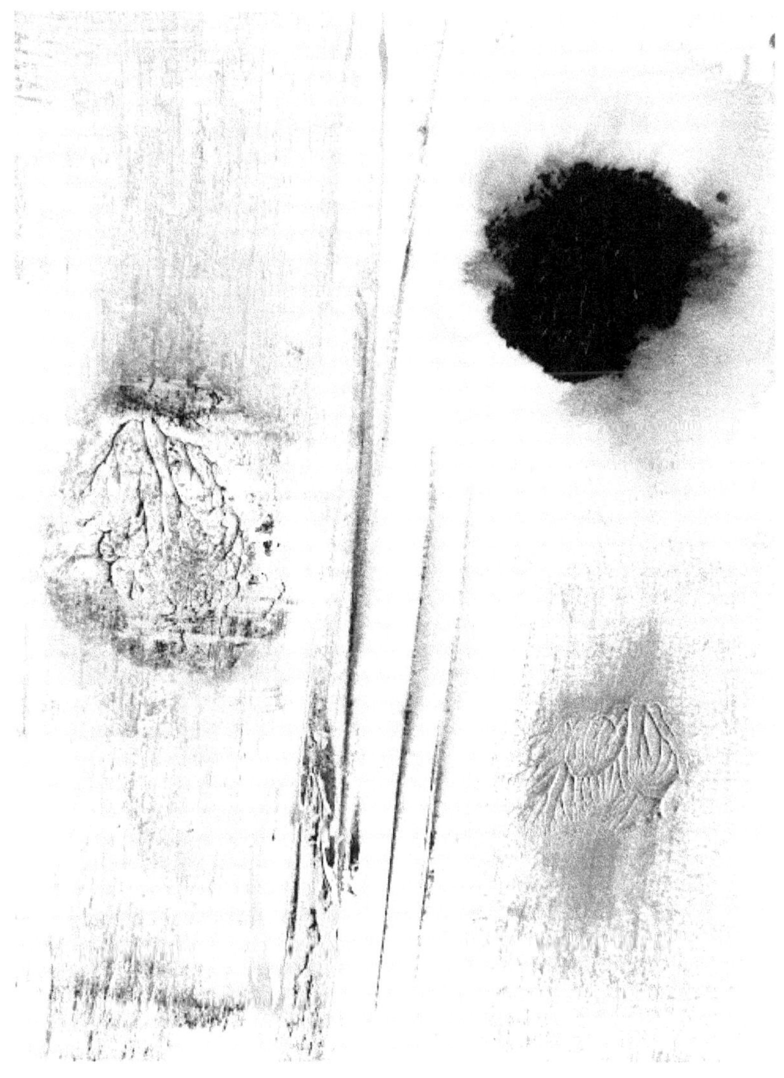

Miss Winter (in 2)

1.

3 minutes of daylight

Gone. Where?

Misplaced like gloves or a friend who moves to your
acquaintance list then fades into the dusk of memory.

I'm writing as fast as I can, to outrun the coming advance. Then
pitched into the coming darkness my face and words obscured
in the umbraed gloom.

And then out of nowhere, Miss Winter arrived, always
unannounced. Always catching me off-guard. We've known
each other for years, but she always remains distant, her
manner always somewhat chilly. But she was a guest.

Would you like some tea?

Yes, that one you served last year. With ice.

I remembered her request and served her
a glass of cooling mint.
With ice.

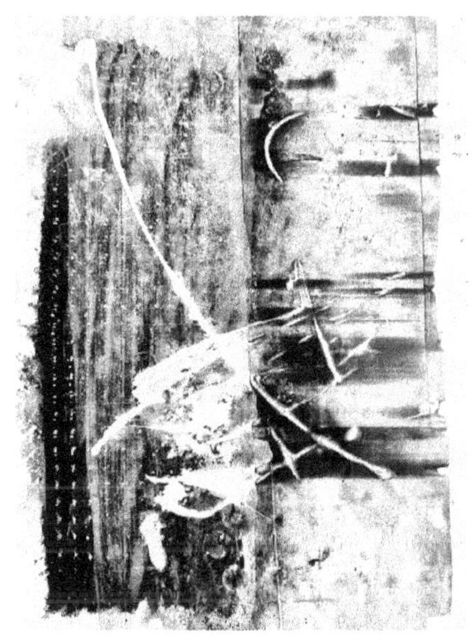

2.

She'd placed a small box wrapped in silver paper with an orange bow on the low table that separated us.

What's this?

A little something. To get you through.

I undid the bow and lifted the lid. Light filled the room.

It's just three minute's worth. I stole it. There'll be another one tomorrow.

And then she was gone. But her presence along with her brisk scent will remain for a dozen weeks.

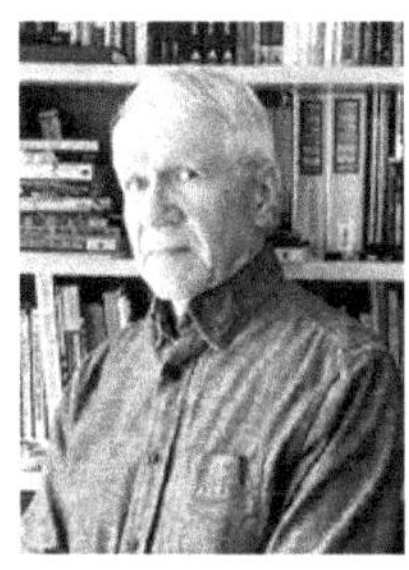

Laurence Carr is a Hudson Valley writer of poetry, fiction and plays. His novel, *Pancake Hollow Primer*, won a Next Generation Indie Book Award. With Codhill Press, he edited *Riverine* and co-edited (with Jan Zlotnik Schmidt) *A Slant of Light: Contemporary Women Writers of the Hudson Valley* (USA Best Book Award for Anthology), Poetry collections include *Paradise Loft* (CAPS Press/Lightwoodpress), *The Wytheport Tales and Threnodies: poems in remembrance*. Over two dozen theatre works have been produced in NYC, throughout the U.S. and in Europe. He collaborated with abstract artist Power Boothe on *Traverse*, an experimental book of art and text. His writing has appeared in numerous publications. Laurence is the publisher of *Lightwood*, an online magazine (Lightwoodpress.com). He is a graduate of Ohio University and New York University and taught Dramatic and Creative Writing at SUNY, New Paltz. www.carrwriter.com

Also by Laurence Carr

Paradise Loft (poems) CAPS Press and Lightwoodpress
Traverse (with artist Power Boothe, text and images) Lightwoodpress
Pancake Hollow Primer (novel in prose and poems) Codhill Press
Threnodies, poems in remembrance (poems) Codhill Press
The Wytheport Tales (poems and prose poems) Codhill Press

Editor: (Codhill Press)
Riverine: an anthology of Hudson Valley Writers
WaterWrites: a Hudson River Anthology (co-editor)
A Slant of Light: Contemporary Women Writers of the Hudson Valley (with Jan Zlotnik Schmidt)
Reflecting Pool: Poets and the Creative Process

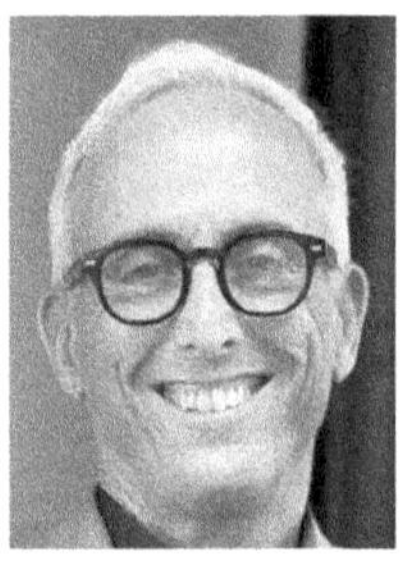

Edward M. O'Hara is a native New Yorker living and creating his artwork in Highland, NY. He studied fine art at CUNY Queens College and the Art Students League. O'Hara's work has been featured at ArtSpace, New Haven, Roost Arts Hudson Valley (debuting its "Creative Conversations" program) and had a solo show at the Wired Gallery in High Falls, NY in 2024.
His is a member of 9W Artists, an eclectic collective of visual artists – all painters – based in the Hudson Valley region of New York State.

Professionally, O'Hara founded SME Branding, a highly successful strategic brand development firm that worked with sports entertainment and higher education brands all over the world. Clients included the United States Olympic Committee, FIFA, World Cup, Adidas, NY Yankees, Kentucky Derby, LPGA, Harvard University, NCAA, ACC, NFL, MLB, NBA and the NHL.

www.oharaart.com, @edohara.art

Edward M. O'Hara Artist Statement
My art is a physical process inciting a metaphysical result. My drawings and paintings avoid all recognizable imagery, allowing the viewer to explore and feel the work without the articulation of a specific narrative. My art intends to connect the audience to their world in a fresh, visceral and emotional way. The work is produced by layering, experimenting, destroying and recreating the surface of the canvas, paper or wood.

I see my art as a membrane through which the viewer passes, revealing notions of the origins of nature, the universe and eternity. I hope my art makes people wonder.

Catalogue of Artwork

CALLING ALL POETS (CO-PUBLISHER)

I have, over the course of CAPS' twenty-five years, employed much hyperbole and eloquent shadings both in the press and in person to discuss our ideals, our perseverance, our ultimate goal. I've hy-per-used such words and vague concepts like democratic forum, free speech, community, camaraderie, open mic, diversity, etc. But when you pare it down, as any poet should, it comes down to one North Star constant.

Tell it. Mean it.
Make us wonder. Make us think.
Make us believe.
Welcome to the fold.

Mike Jurkovic - Prez, Calling All Poets Series and CAPS Press
Greg Correll, Book design and IT

Also published by CAPS Press

CAPS 25th Anniversary Anthology,
edited by the CAPS Editorial Board

Paradise Loft, poems by Laurence Carr,
CAPS Press/ LIghtwoodpress

CAPS Poetry 2020 Anthology,
edited by Roger Aplon

EKPHRASIS 2020 Poetry + Images,
(Exhibition February 7- March 1, 2020)

CAPS Poetry 2015 Anthology,
edited by Marina Mati

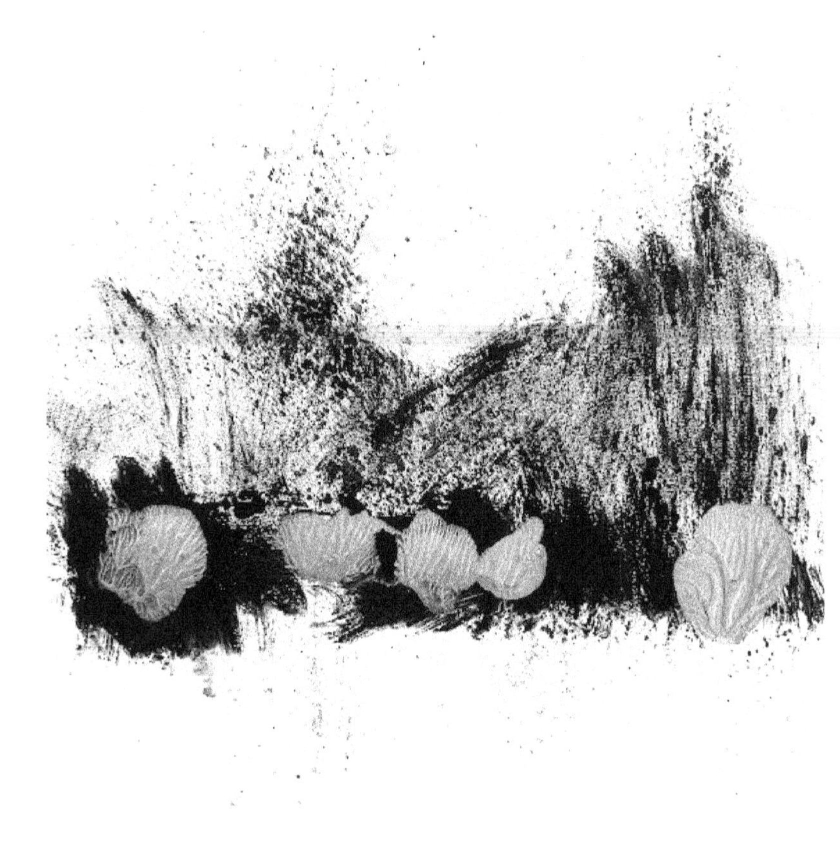

STRIDES

reflections on 6 acres
by Laurence Carr

artwork by Edward M. O'Hara